GW01280662

Tricia Osborne's

Green and Pleasant Land

A colouring book nature trail
through countryside and garden

Matador
9 Priory Business Park,
Wistow Road, Kibworth Beauchamp,
Leicestershire. LE8 0RX
Tel: 0116 279 2299
Email: books@troubador.co.uk
Web: www.troubador.co.uk/matador
Twitter: @matadorbooks

ISBN 978 1788037 464

British Library Cataloguing in Publication Data.
A catalogue record for this book is available from the British Library.

Printed and bound in the UK by TJ International, Padstow, Cornwall
Typeset by Troubador Publishing Ltd, Leicester, UK

Matador is an imprint of Troubador Publishing Ltd

MIX
Paper from responsible sources
FSC® C013056

This book belongs to

Welcome

Follow the nature trail as you
embark on a countryside ramble
and take a stroll in the garden.
Discover animals, birds,
insects and flowers.
Bring the pages to life as you
fill them with colour.
I hope you enjoy this journey
and find as much pleasure
as I have in creating
them for you.

A COUNTRYSIDE RAMBLE
RIGHT OF WAY

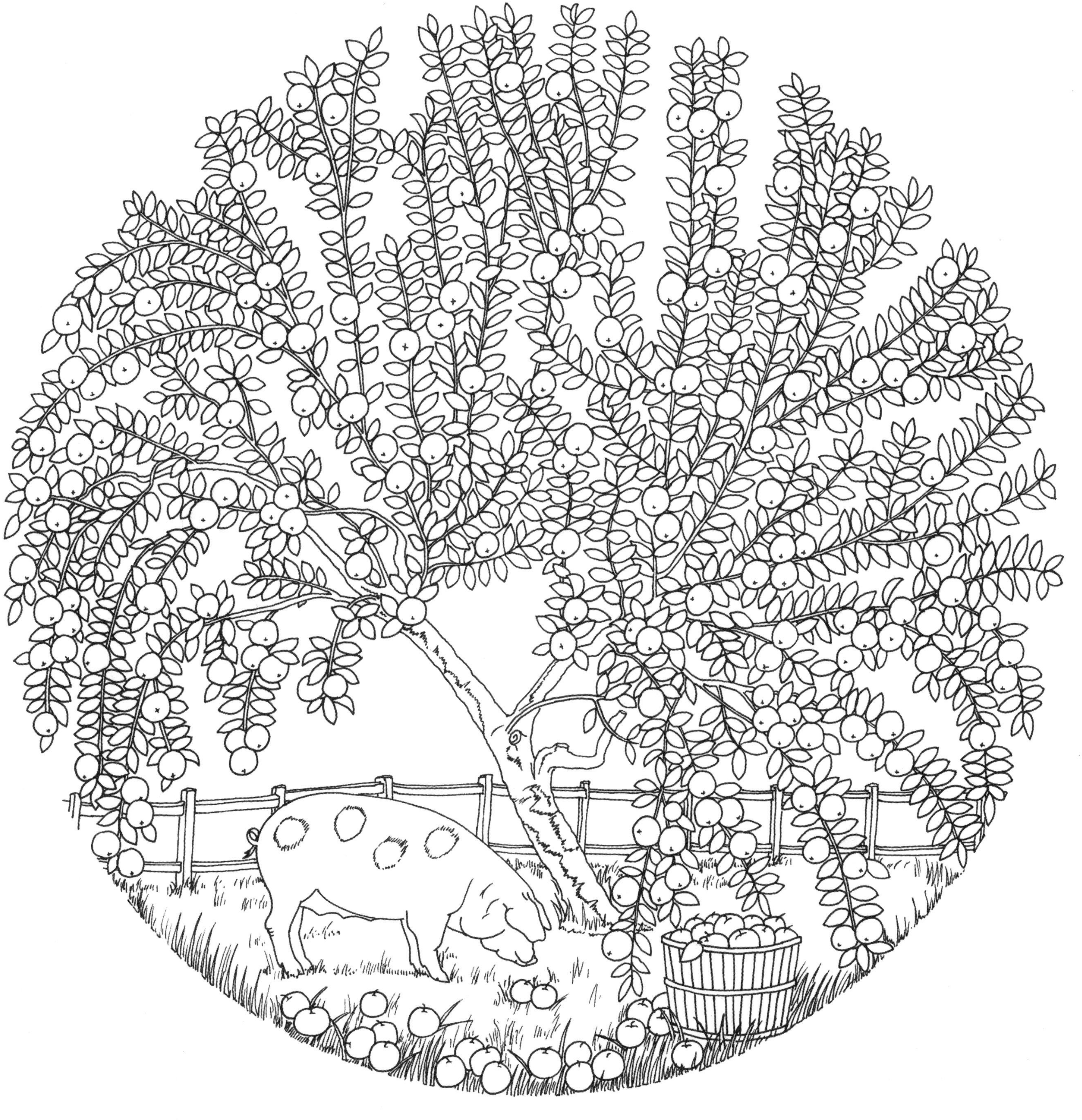

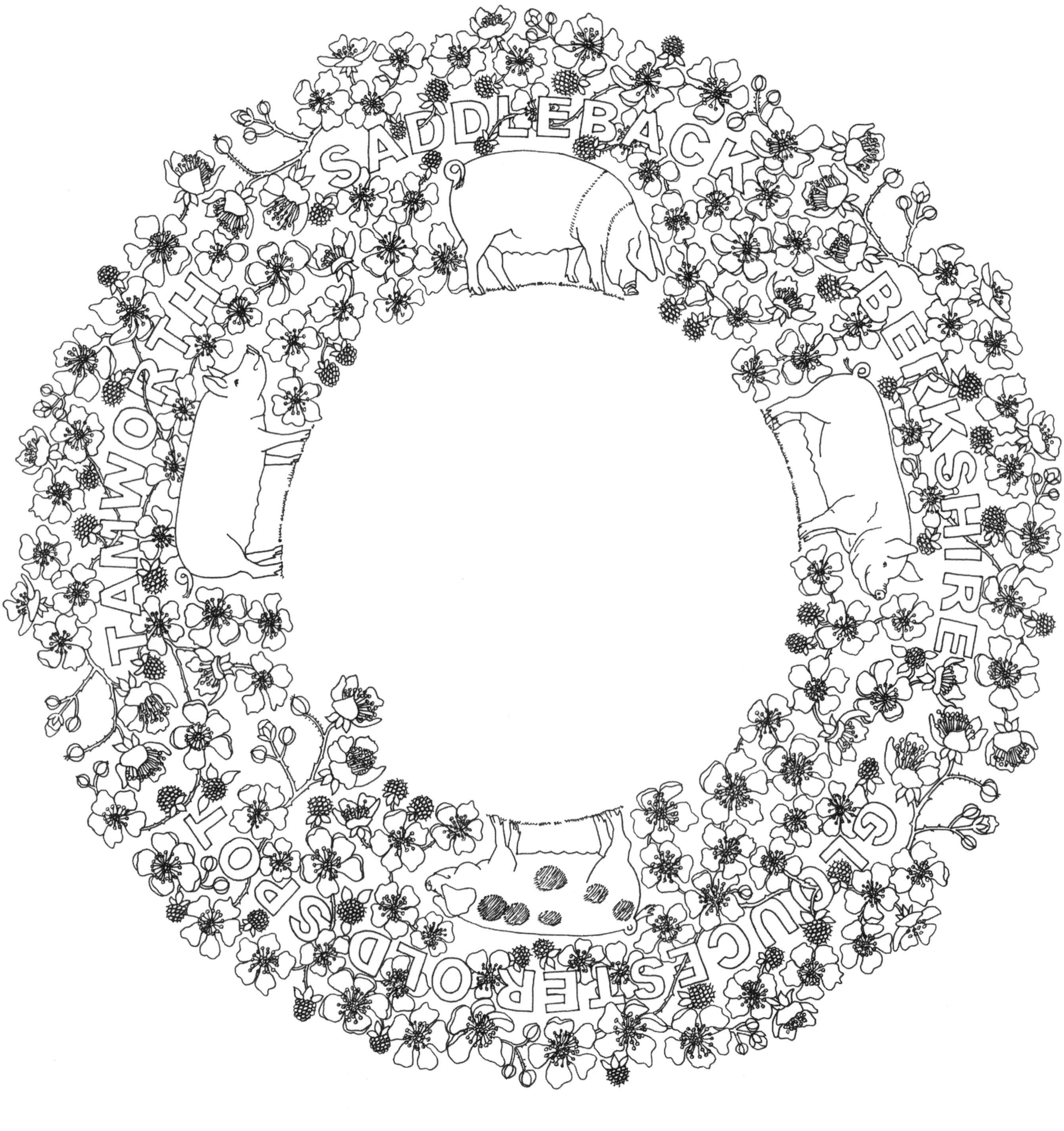
SADDLEBACK
BERKSHIRE
GLOUCESTER OLD SPOT
TAMWORTH

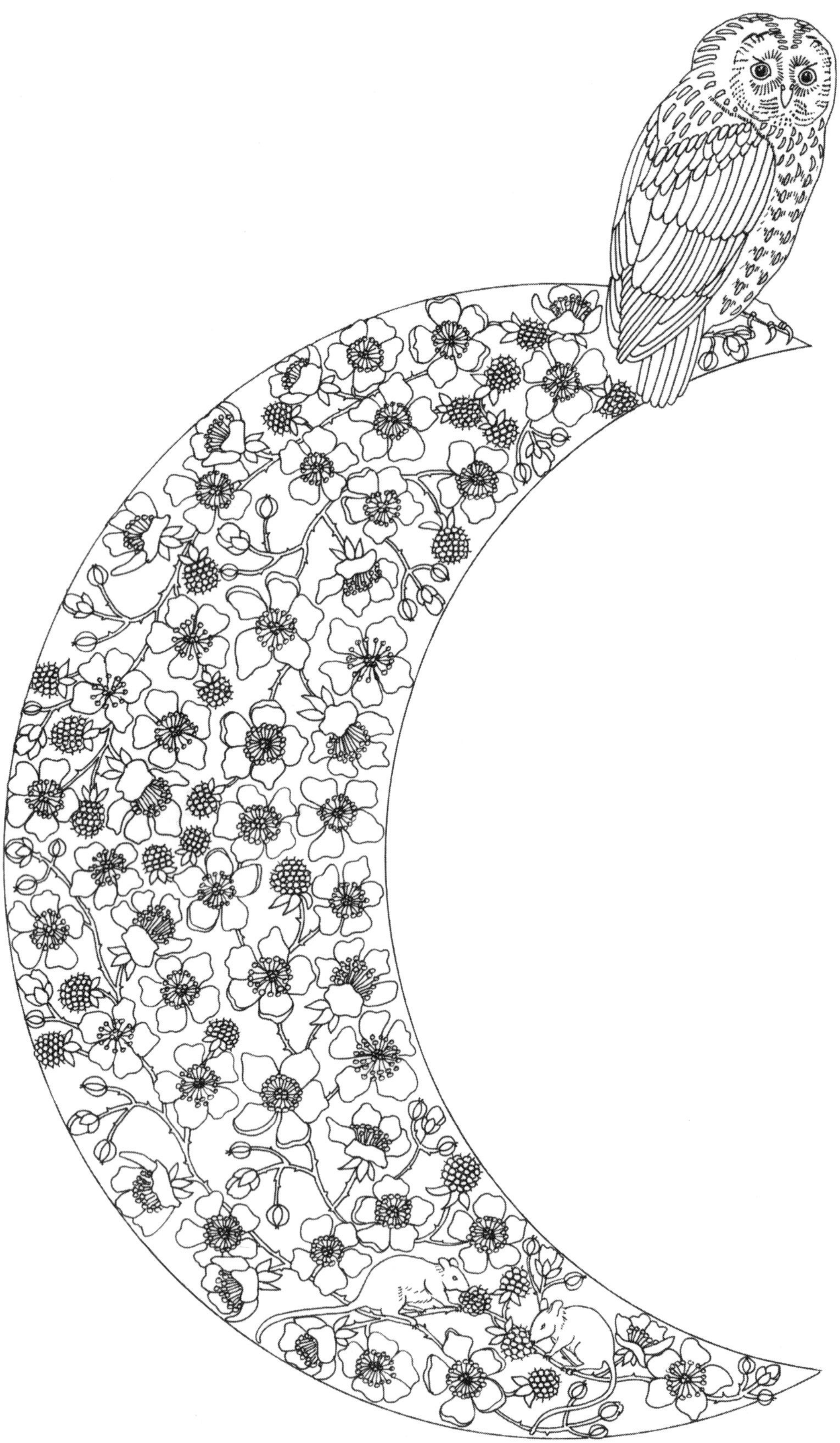

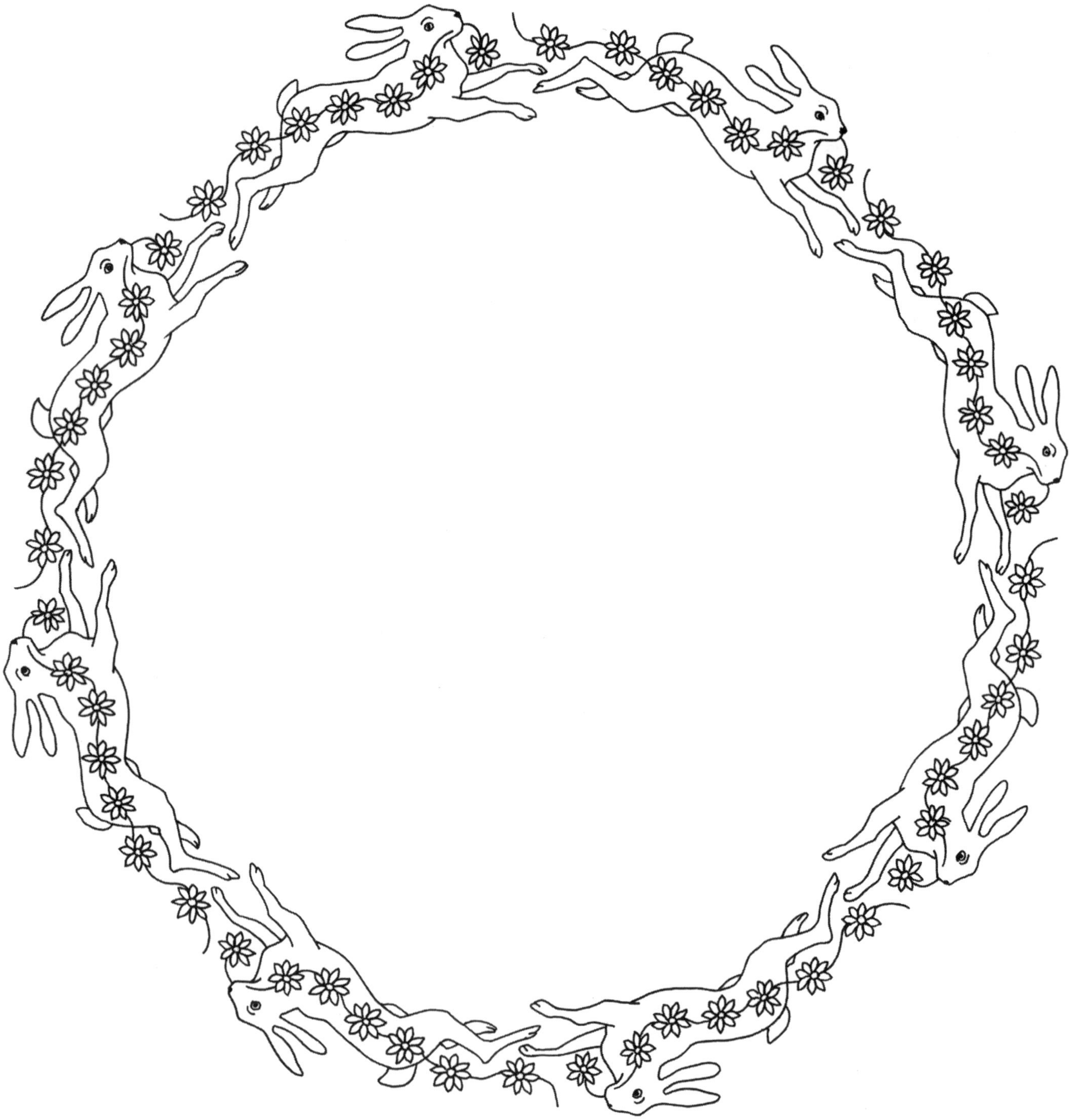

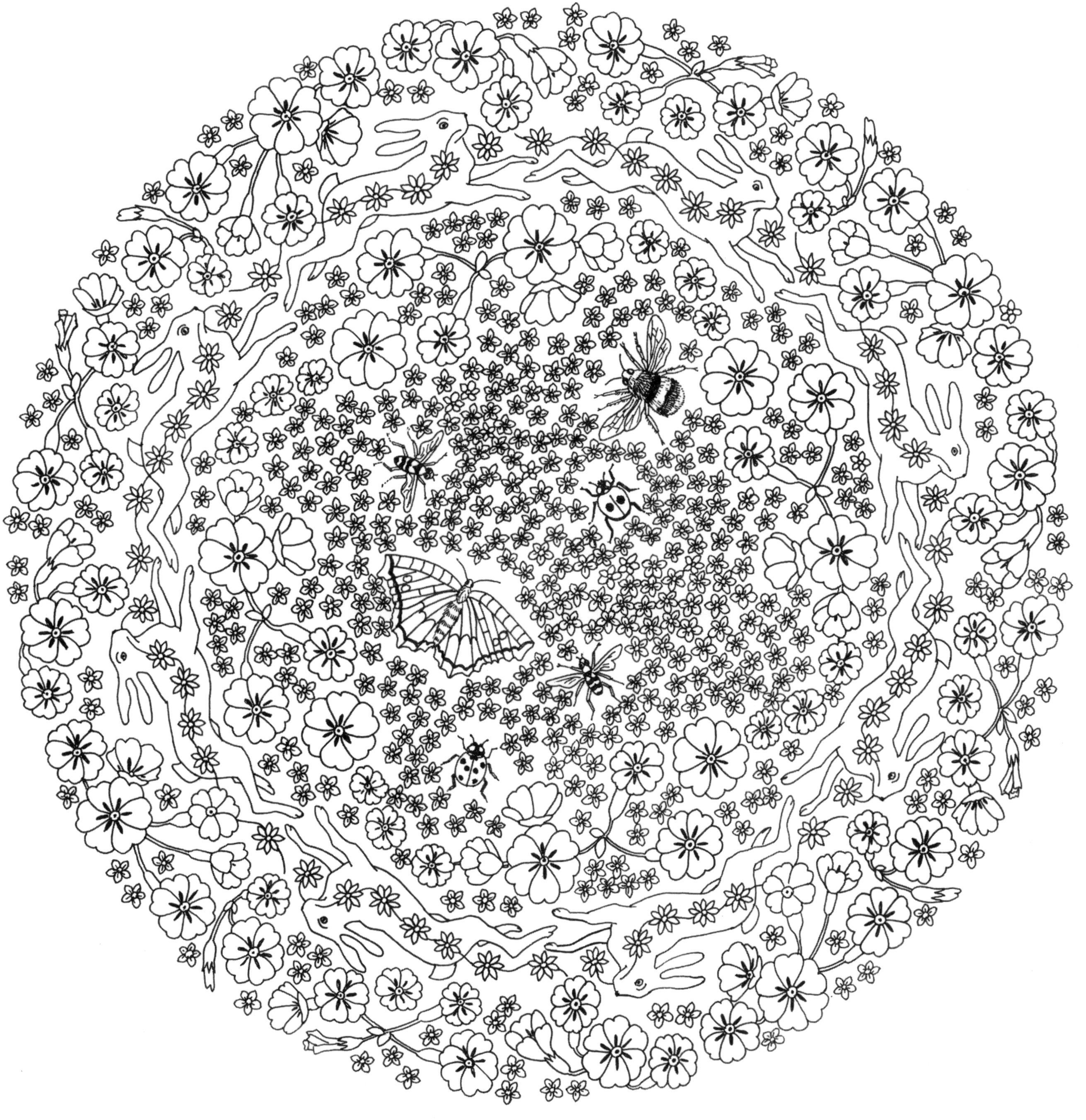

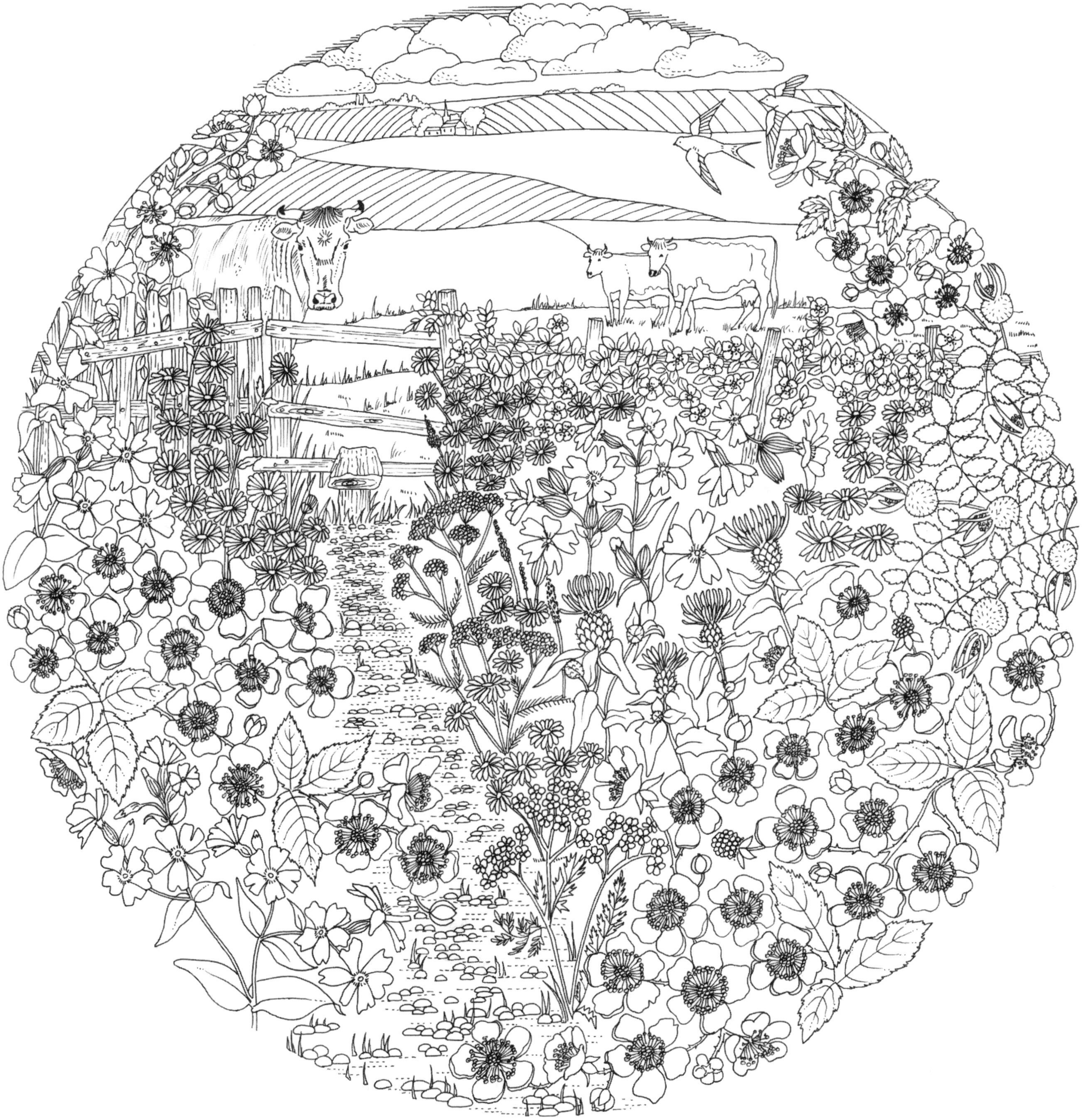

A STROLL IN THE GARDEN

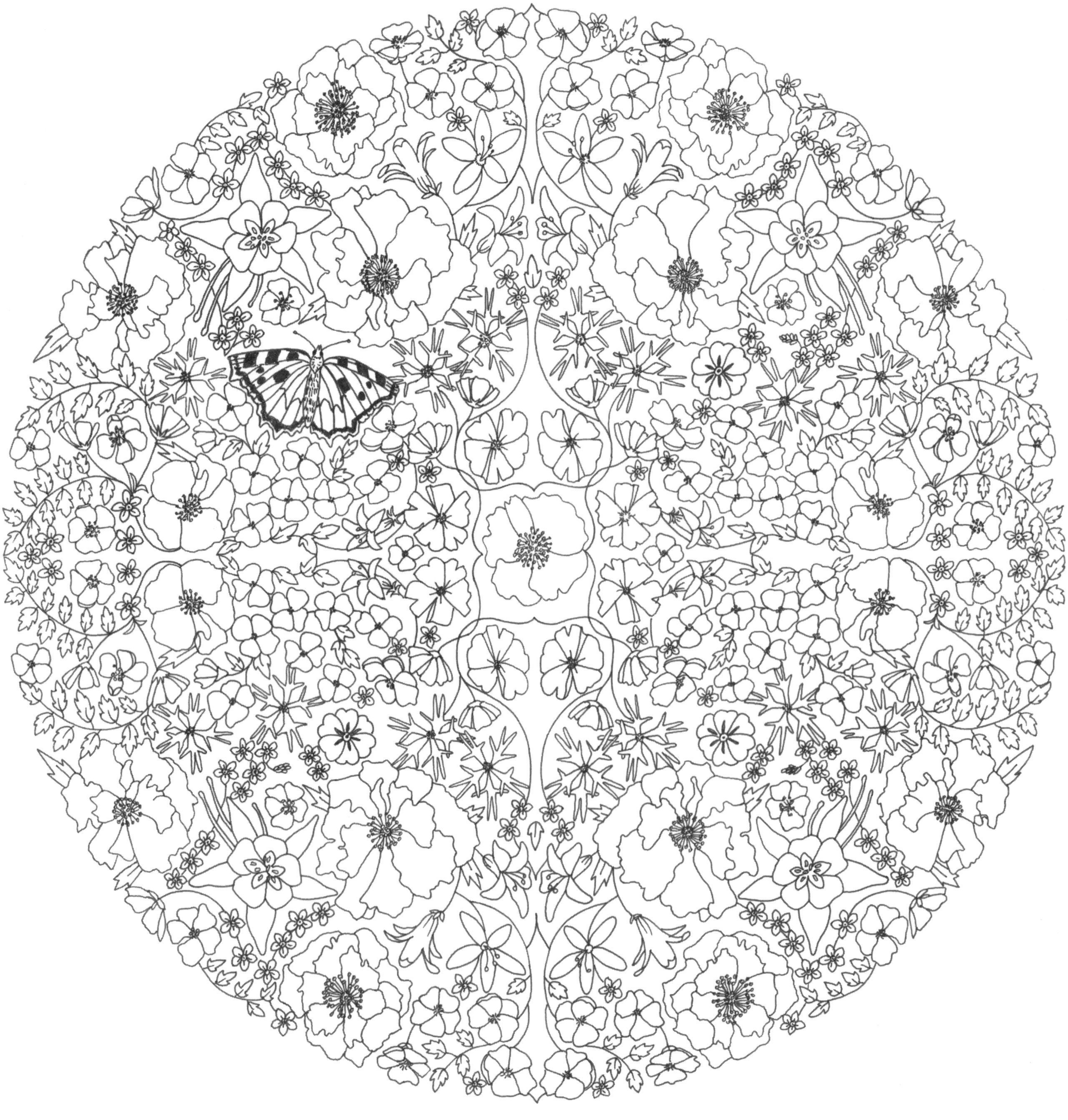

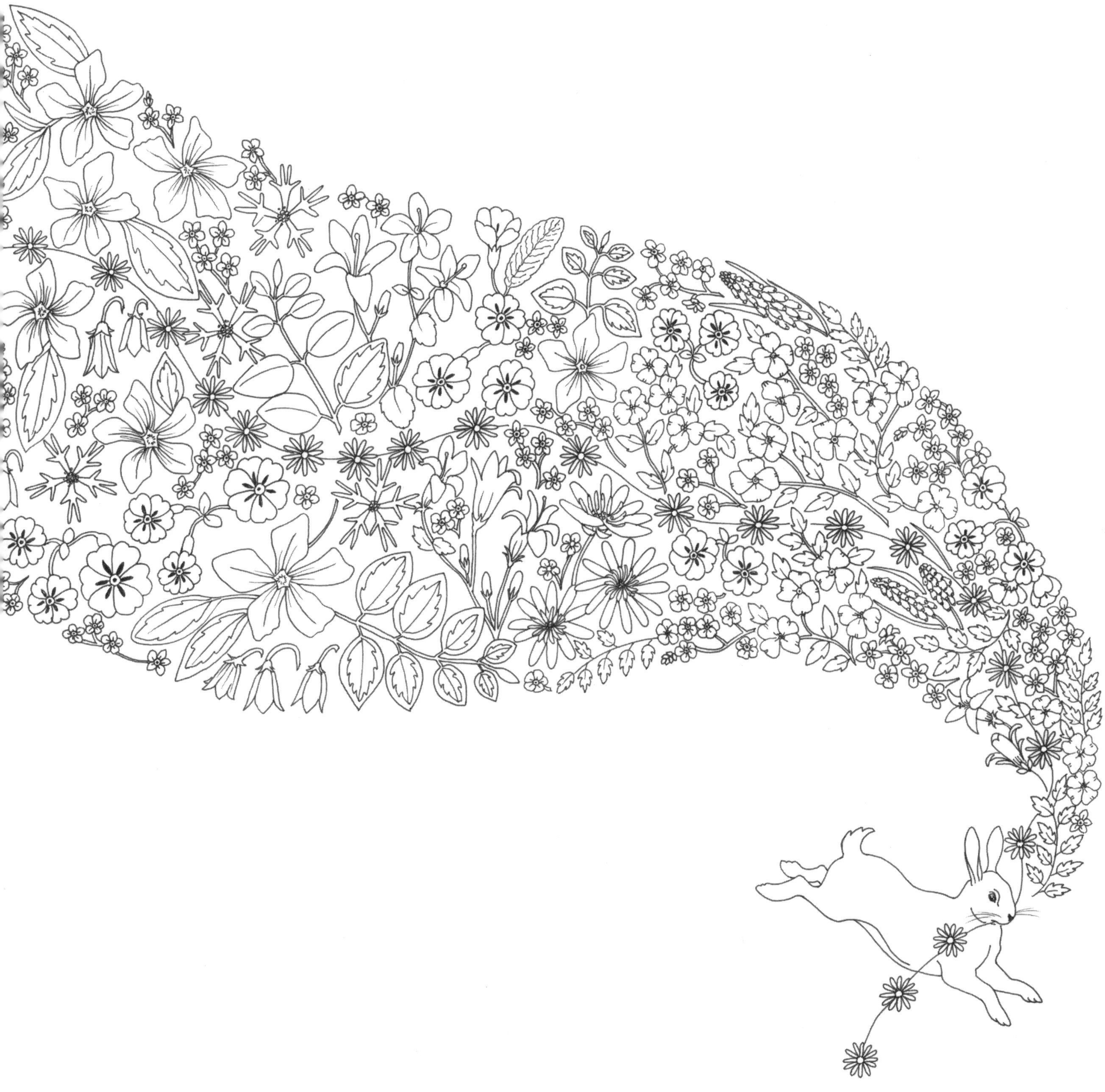

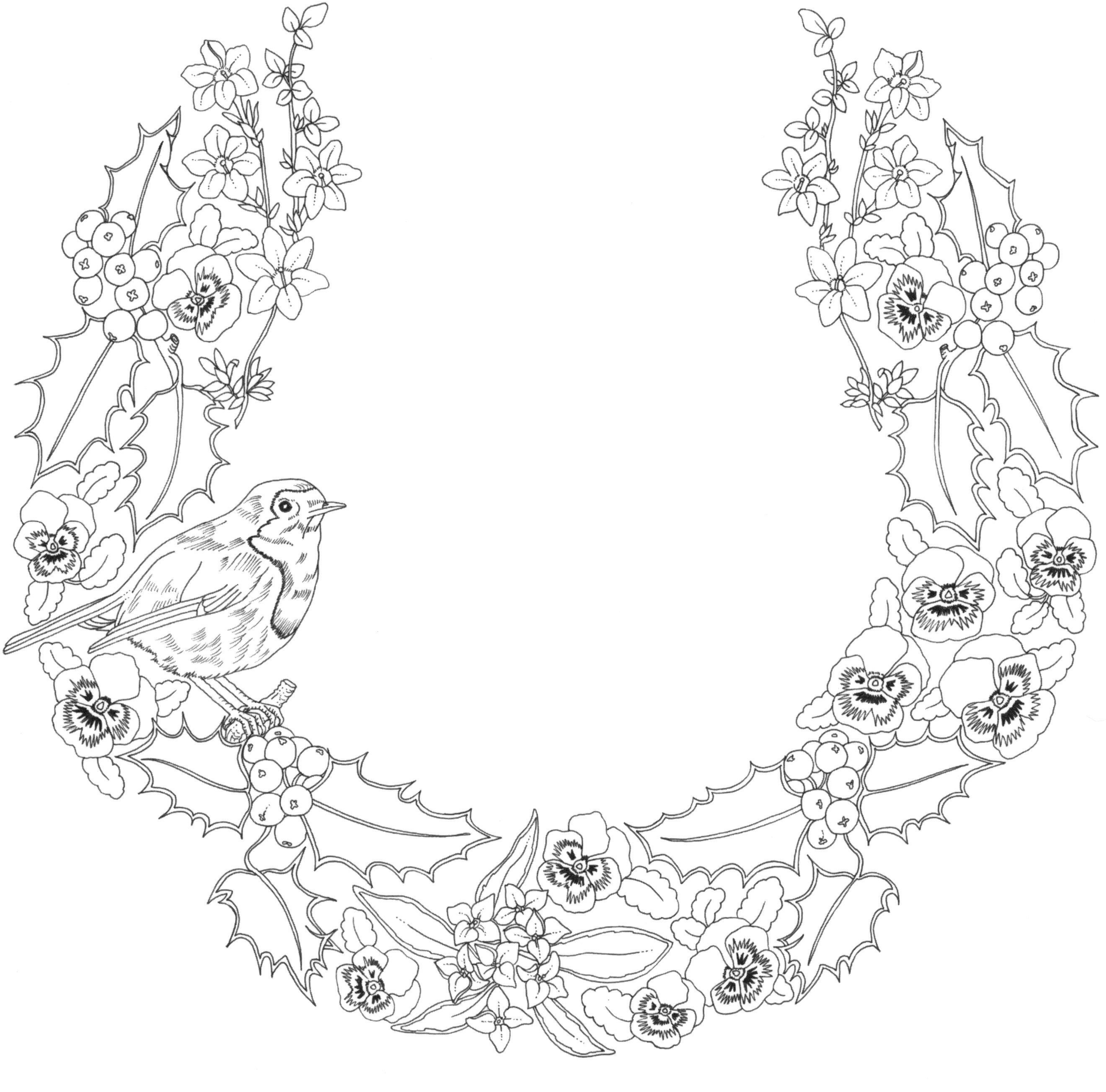

THEN RELAX WITH A NICE CUP OF TEA